Wilderness Light

Wilderness Light

Switzerland Rediscovered
Photographs by Max Schmid

Essay by
Urs Frauchiger

EDITION STEMMLE

Zurich New York

Contents

The Picture as a Musical Score

Urs Frauchiger

The Sound Arenas of Switzerland

This is not a book to be merely glanced at. You need to get inside Max Schmid's photographs. And it is only once you are inside, that they will start to resonate.

In this age of multimedia, where pictures are forever accompanied by sounds and narration, and where musical compositions are illustrated and commented on until their effect is ruined, this is a unique experience. Suddenly we remember that art has always been a multimedia phenomenon. We, as the beholders, the listeners, and the "readers" in the broadest sense of the term are the ones who establish the connections. No one can pre-determine for us, or even dictate to us, which sounds the pictures will evoke in us, or which pictures will inspire which sounds. These come from our own anthology of experiences and belong to us alone. They are our active contribution to the adventurous and mysterious process of "perceiving" art, and they transcend mere consumption.

As soon as the magic word is uttered, the world starts to sing. This is certainly true at least if real magic is not confused with simple conjuring, trickery or sleight of hand. The magic results from the patience with which Max Schmid tracks down these phenomena and the precision with which he captures them at just the right moment, perhaps the one and only moment. That instant when the matrix of ancient and future structures appears beneath or behind the surface of the landscape and reverberates.

If the term "myth" had not been used with such wanton abandon, we ought really to speak of a mythical occurrence. And it is precisely this abandon that Max Schmid drives out in his photographs. His pictures have nothing to do with the customary myths of the perfect mountain landscape, a landscape which is both stared at and which stares back in all its photogenic dignity. On the contrary, these pictures satisfy Albrecht Dürer's exacting demand of what a picture should be, namely "inwardly full of form," and they capture the resoundingly turbulent shape of the landscape.

We have grown accustomed to regarding the Alps as something majestically unshakable, something eternal, a high-lying Arcadia, a stronghold of freedom, the tower looking down over Europe's battles, and a veritable fortress. The Alps promise security, protection and self-confidence—sometimes too much. Indeed, in excess, these qualities are transformed into superciliousness, into the desire to hide away from the world, into indignation and the inability to perceive and understand other ways of life.

The nation-states that were formed within and on the periphery of the Alps during the 19th century wisely fashioned their image on these colossal massifs. The prominent peaks were easily remembered icons for self-promotion both internally and externally. They evinced profound historical action; they provided a guarantee of endurance and reliability; they served as staffage for the ideas of the German idealism of democracy, justice and a perfect world, and as settings for Biedermeier idylls and romantic sketches.

And so it was that the myth grew both from experiences lived and also from the evaluation of outsiders. The Alps became a subject for painters and subsequently photographers. The picture became detached from direct contemplation of the scene. Siegfried Kracauer wrote: "The public sees the world through journals, but it is these same journals that impede our perception of the world." The Alpine dweller who was pictured, that same person who was stared at by tourists, started to act the part of himself and to play the role that others wanted to see him playing, rather than being himself. Down below, in those twee village-like Swiss towns, an artificial alpine world was created. Arolla-pine furniture and wobbly stools found their way into apartments, while geraniums adorned the concrete ledges. As soon as the town-dwellers returned home from the office, they squeezed themselves into their herdsmen's jackets and headed for the local yodeling club to celebrate in song the springtime return of the herds to the mountains and the pure quality of mountain life. Suddenly there was talk of identity—something that only happens when that same identity starts to slip away from one's grasp. The older generation clung to the myth, while the younger generation destroyed it in panic and sounded off about globalization.

One would assume that of all people the Alpine dwellers should know just how easily avalanches and landslides can be triggered off, and how in most cases those responsible are the first casualties. But we do not destroy the Alpine myth by destroying the Alps. There is also no point in mentioning that only a tiny percentage of those living in the Alps now farm the land.

Anyone who resides in the Alpine area is a farmer by definition, a former mountain farmer perhaps who has now descended geographically to the lowlands. Although his descent was mostly allied to an ascent in material terms, he has certainly not escaped the Alps. The Alps are always there, somewhere, on the fringe of our horizons. They shimmer audaciously in their morning splendor, they glow melodramatically at dusk, and they appear at unreal distances or loom intrusively before our windows in the crystal-clear föhn-laden air. Whether we flee from them or return to them, we still have to skirt round their crevasses, go through them or scale them. In short, they keep us moving while keeping moving themselves.

The Dynamics of the Alps

It is a sign of an unbelievable reduction of the time scale that we perceive the Alps as the embodiment of something static. There is nothing more dynamic than those masses, washed here some 100 million years ago in Tethys Sea by mighty rivers, folding upwards with powerful thrusts; masses that intertwined and slid over each other. Underneath the patient force of erosion, debris formed and furrowing occurred. Older layers were exposed and rocks molded until the magma, at the mercy of varying pressures, gathered momentum again and burst through the mountains above, turning them inside out. Tranquillity has never really dwelt here. The Alps are full of inner tension that they unleash from time to time in tectonic tremors, or in occurrences that we usually describe as catastrophes. We consider them thus because we insist on the static view. We perceive the immense movement, the roaring and crashing, the falling of rocks, snow and water, the irrepressibility of the wind and fire as a disturbance of the surface, and not as the fundamental movement of that space.

So could this agreeable stability of the Alpine culture, the preserving, the persisting, the rituals, the customs, the costumes and that sense of striving for something in all good faith be merely self-deception? Certainly not. Only those who trust the moment can survive in such dynamics. Neither the chamois nor its hunter would have wended their way along the bands of rock with instinctive sureness if they had not had faith in their continued existence. The world is exactly as we encounter it. Ask a local how long this chapel has been here or that oak tree there on the ridge, and he will answer: "Oh, it was always there." He is perfectly right, for when he was born, in other words, when his world was created, it was there. This has nothing to do with narrow-mindedness or limited intelligence. On the contrary, it is a pragmatic answer to the certainty that the time we have measured is in any event disproportionate. It is too short for eternity and too long for a razor-sharp decisive moment.

The great travelers who ventured into the wilderness viewed the confidence of the Alpine dweller as idyllic, but scarcely as a survival strategy in an unforgiving environment. Albrecht von Haller described this as a pre-civilisational ideal state; while Goethe spoke of the occasionally burdensome yet still sweet bliss in the "silent pastoral dwelling"—an Alpine counterpart to his Weimar summer house, so to speak. Seume, on the other hand, who was a walker, considered it "the ultimate pleasure to be able to hike in the Alps year in year out." For Rousseau's part, his yearning for "Nature" was in any event a phantom; one that he thought he could sense through the curtains of his salon.

One traveler was clearly overawed by the enormity of the Alps. In June 1831, Felix Mendelssohn wrote from Chamonix:

"People had tried to persuade me that it was my imagination that made the mountains appear larger, but yesterday at sunset I paced up and down in front of the house. Every time I turned my back on the mountains, I attempted to picture those masses as vividly as I could. And every time I turned around again, they were there, far in excess of how I had imagined them. Words, pictures and thoughts are all too insignificant here. It is only when you see it with your own eyes that you can picture it. (...) I spent the whole of today in peace and quite alone. I wanted to draw the view of the mountains but, on opening my book, I found the page so very small that I did not even feel like starting at first. Only later did I decide to scale everything down to my eye."

When the then 22-year-old wandered through the Swiss Alps alone, he was one of the few to realize that, although he was lauded as a wonder of the world by his own illustrious contemporaries, he was the lesser being in this macrocosm. Without hesitation, this man, who was also endowed with considerable talent for writing and drawing, and who was able to handle these gifts with remarkable oversight, opted not to attempt to monopolize these Alps for himself in any ideological or aesthetic sense. Not only was his page too small to achieve this, but also his terms of reference too limited. Thus, in an act of good sense and wisdom, he had to take them back to his own dimensions.

As it happened, he experienced this mountain world in "the most catastrophic of conditions." The dynamics of the Alps, as described above, made themselves known to him in frightening fashion that summer: storms raged, and water gushed down from the mountains destroying paths and bridges, and sweeping fields and farms down into the depths. Villages were flooded and whole valley communities cut off from the surroundings. Mendelssohn negotiated all of this with the fleetness of a chamois, covering distances in a day that would command anyone's respect for his obvious peak physical condition. With his watchful eye, he, as a master of delicate sentiment but never sentimental, felt compassion. In the evenings, he dried himself out while composing, playing the organ, and helping at church services. In addition, he kept himself informed of the similarly turbulent state of the world by reading Swiss newspapers, which he described as "so full of holes, with faltering prose, and loosely composed," and which reminded him of a "Swiss log road." He also read *William Tell* on the way with a loving perceptiveness—and this allowed him to record and understand the flaws.

However, when he saw others showing indifference or even arrogance, this well-educated son of a banker and grandson of an eminent philosopher, was gripped by sudden rage. This same rage did not even allow him to spare his admired mentor:

> "That Goethe was not able to compose anything more than a few inferior poems and letters that were of even poorer quality while he was in Switzerland is as much a mystery to me as many other things in this world."

The affected behaviour on the part of tourists, which had apparently remained unchanged for more than a century and a half, enraged him still further:

> "When I see how people pass through Switzerland and find nothing special about it, in the same way as they find nothing special about anything—apart from themselves; how they are not at all stirred nor shaken; how they can even remain aloof and act like Philistines when gazing upon the mountains—I could hit them. Two Englishmen are sitting here beside me and there is an Englishwoman up near the stove; they are more wooden than sticks. (...) They have not even mentioned that there are mountains here. Travelling for them means scolding the guide—who mocks them—quarrelling with the innkeepers, and yawning with one another."

Shaken and Stirred or Aloof and Philistine?

Apart from the precision and dexterity of his prose, what makes Mendelssohn's letters so relevant to today is his intelligent and emotional observation. Those true-to-life postcard pictures and the advertising art which have long characterized Switzerland's image appear fresh, unadulterated and almost avant-garde to us, and so too does Mendelssohn's writing. Like many musicians, Mendelssohn commanded an almost cinematic vista. On one of the few fine-weather days during his stay, he made his way up to Kleine Scheidegg with a guide from Grindelwald. On the way, they heard that a celebration was taking place on one of the high-lying Alps and decided to embark on the considerable detour. An alpine herdsman pointed out the route to them:

> "The herdsman was a barbaric fellow, who was always running on ahead like a cat. (...) The path was terribly steep, but he praised it because he usually took a shorter, steeper route. Although our herdsman was around 60, whenever my younger guide and I had reached the top of a hill, we saw the fellow already descending the next one.
>
> For two hours, we followed the most grueling route that I have ever encountered. We climbed high and then dropped all the way down again, over boulders, across streams, ditches, and a few snowfields, in utmost solitude. There were no paths and no sign of anything man-made. Occasionally we could still hear the avalanches from the Jungfrau. Otherwise, it was silent."

Finally they reached the summit and

> "all of a sudden saw crowds of people standing in a circle, talking, laughing, calling out. All of them were in colorful costumes with flowers on their hats; there were numerous girls, a number of bar tables with wine casks, and all around the deep silence and those awesome mountains."

He gazed down into the misty depths, where he saw

> "all those tiny waterfalls, houses looking like dots, and trees like grass."

And then the celebration:

> "They were wrestling, singing, arguing and laughing—all of them able, honest and healthy individuals. I thoroughly enjoyed the 'Schwingen,' the traditional wrestling—something I had never

seen before. Then the girls served the men kirsch and schnapps. The bottles passed from hand to hand and I drank with the people. Three small children were delighted when I handed each of them some cake, and a very inebriated old farmer sang a song for me. Then they all sang, including my guide, who performed a modern song very proficiently. Afterwards, two small boys started to fight. Everything I saw on that Alp I thoroughly enjoyed."

After his descent from the mountain through a fresh glacial wind, he reviewed his day:

"It is already late and the avalanches can still be heard from time to time. Well, that was my Sunday. Quite some feast indeed!"

The Mountain Resonance Arena

It is striking how little the musician Mendelssohn speaks of music in his writing. But then again, his writing emits its own sound. His Alpine sphere is a sound arena in which silence has sound; occasionally a word of endearment from him, occasionally a distant rustling, roaring, whistling, and thudding—and a tinkling. Intermingled with this is the sound of birdsong. The sound picture is, in fact, more reminiscent of Minimal music than of Mendelssohn's own compositions. And the people sing; they sing with such naturalness that it is hardly worthy of mention. They simply sing.

Mendelssohn refrained from passing any judgement; neither did he embark on lengthy descriptions, nor did he see fit to judge or describe the call of the birds.

Music in the Alpine regions always takes the form of singing, or more precisely of calling: calling to someone, calling home, or calling for help. The sound of speech, namely conveying information in the broadest and most pragmatic sense. *Kuhreihen* was a song used to drive the cows: an useful way of bringing cattle back into the cowshed as rapidly as possible. Yodeling, for its part, was originally a pure expression of love of life (or of life's sufferings), a free improvisation on a series of well-worn phrases that were joyously shouted out. These were then handed down through generations, much like a birdcall and, like the birdcall, they sometimes attracted, sometimes warned, or sometimes indicated territory. The archaic form of prayer, in which the herdsman called to the Virgin Mary and the Saints through a wooden horn at dawn, has reached cosmic heights. This prayer call has survived the influence of tourist folklore because it was never relegated to the level of a ritual carried out for a purpose other than its original one. Since Rousseau's time, *Kuhreihen* has become a symbol for homesickness and subsequently as a mark of affected folk tradition. Only in the 19th century did natural yodeling give way to the singing of yodeling songs. This form is, however, more familiar in the lowlands and in the towns and cities (and the media) than it is in the mountains.

There were, of course, instruments as well. These began with *Arte povera* that used everyday objects converted into instruments to produce music, in the same way as children do. This is in no way meant to belittle this activity; on the contrary, it was a genuine reaction arising from the spontaneous joy in expression and innovation. And we are now discovering this power again in the music-making of cultures outside of Europe. The broom held against the shoulder served as an "Alpine man's drum." This was supplemented by whip cracking, by the rhythmic beating of wooden spoons, and by the sharp metallic contours of two soup spoons held between the fingers and sounded against every imaginable part of the body. This was body music, a practice that is now admired as an innovative form of expression in performances on the international Off Scene. Nasal singing through a silk-wrapped comb served as a substitute for the prohibitively expensive mouth-organ centuries before Ennio Morricone blew his far-reaching melodies of yearning into the vast rocky landscapes of the Wild West. Likewise, cowbells rang out or resounded through the echo caverns of the rocky mountain arena.

There is also very early evidence of specific musical instruments. The folk music researcher, Brigitte Bachmann-Geiser, speaks of discoveries of Jewish harps and bones that produced a buzzing sound dating from the 13th century, and of a type of Alpine horn hollowed out of a young fir tree around 1400. The dulcimer was mentioned as early as 1446. Shortly afterwards came the stringed instruments, then zithers, which were often used as an accompaniment for roving minstrels and singers of the time. Soldiers returning from military campaigns brought drums and pipes along with them, while the invading French left behind the Turkish crescent, which they had taken from the janizaries.

It is not possible for us even to begin to imagine the extent of variety and variability of different sound sources and equipment used to produce sound. However, our forebears, with their emotive nature, their curiosity and their joy of discovery played their part in this. In addition, there was the gradual but long-lasting exchange of cultures brought about by those returning home and those passing through. These included soldiers, merchants, craftsmen, milkers and hired hands who took work where they found it, as well as laborers who crossed the borders of neighboring lands in search of employment. Then there were those first droll figures who came to visit the mountains just for the sake of doing so. These travelers brought with them musical forms and methods of music-making from advanced civilizations. And, in turn, these advanced civilizations were enriched through their unadulterated love of discovery by taking on board what was only later to be known as "folk music."

If we try, in our inner imagination, to reconstruct the sound picture of the Alps, we see that it is not that viscous, "fresh from the cow" folklore sound, which is a far more recent phenomenon than it might care to imagine. On the contrary, it is a world of endless complexity within a deep, mysterious and also frightening silence, from which bursts forth the archaic roaring, crashing and blowing; apocalyptic howling, the ostinato intoning of the stones. And, inside all of this, there is the rhythmised everyday communication of people, with their leisure-time songs and dances. And, again and again, those lonely calls out into the universe.

Those elements that we think we are discovering or inventing in electronic recording studios, on sound mixers and in alternative sound processes have always existed in the Alpine area.

Seeing Sound

Contemporary musicians have not really rediscovered this sound world yet. Granted, Alpine instruments are being included in "New Music," in jazz and in rock. There are crossovers and media-friendly multi-cultural sessions, where musicians are flown in from every corner of the globe to arrive at the lowest common denominator with their audiences—and make fools of themselves in doing so. And they entertain the illusion that they are communicating, something that they might just about be able to achieve with a lifetime's effort. And there is Cyrill Schläpfer's cult film, *Ur-Musig* (*Primeval Music*), which made "authentic folk music" accessible to the masses. But this was a phenomenon beyond music itself. Musically speaking, there was nothing new in the film apart from the fact that the volume bordered on the decibel level of a rock concert. What was new for most people were the landscapes, especially the facial landscapes, in which the music is formed and reflected with unexpected passion and power.

And that brings us back to the picture, to Mendelssohn and to Max Schmid's photographs. I have seldom seen pictures that resonate as much. They are musical scores, but more forceful and more precise and subtle than conventional musical notation. They are also more readable. The great archaic signs and movements: the mountains, the snow, the water, the ice, the sky, the clouds, and the horizon. And contained within all of that is a fine structure, in which we can lose ourselves for ever: the microcosm of the lichens and grasses, of the rocks, of the waves, of the clouds, and of the wind, and their reflections in the unending variety of light. His pictures exclude the Switzerland that is too often seen in glorious weather on picture postcard views. There is great calmness in these pictures, but nothing static. It is that calmness which gives birth to breath, to wind, to the weather, to storms—and to sound.

There is great wisdom in this approach to landscape. A patience that reacts instantaneously when the moment is there. This cannot be compared with a "snapshot," or with easy prey that is quickly caught and devoured, or even less with a view of an ideal world that has to be captured before it sinks into banality again. No. The essence here is to capture the moment when subjective feeling and objective seeing become one; the moment when the mystery reveals a small part of itself; the moment when what Hegel described as the "sensory appearance of the idea" flickers up.

When I first saw Max Schmid's pictures, I could not help but compare them with the paintings of Caspar David Friedrich. In the meantime, I have gathered from the already substantial literature on the photographer that I am not the only one to have made this comparison. Perhaps the comparison is not an accurate one. It does, however, probably do justice to the feeling of nature that seeks the eternal in the fleeting moment. It seems to me, though, that Max Schmid refrains from resorting to Friedrich's demiurgical grasp of a scene. Friedrich creates a new world out of the pieces of a set that make up what really exists; Schmid's access is at once humbler and more demanding. He captures that which really exists, that which convinces him, that which overpowers; that which is right in itself.

No one should come and ask where the overhead power lines are, or the motorways, or the overdeveloped and spoiled landscapes. Schmid steers clear of the accusatory and militantly fundamentalist approach. Now and then one can lose oneself in a dark forest lake, only to find, on closer examination, that it is in fact an artificial lake. But artificial lakes can be attractive as well. Not once do we catch him transfiguring, arranging or deceiving. There is the world of his pictures, and he helps us to find them and to see them. Only when we perceive that the world is indestructible and believe in that concept will we want to prevent its destruction.

And when we know its sound. Perhaps pictures will be the most important sound-carriers of the future. At the close of Mendelssohn's letters quoted above, in which he slated the tourists, he said:

> "Someone else would thank God that he could see all of this. And
> I want to be that someone else."

Max Schmid is that someone else.

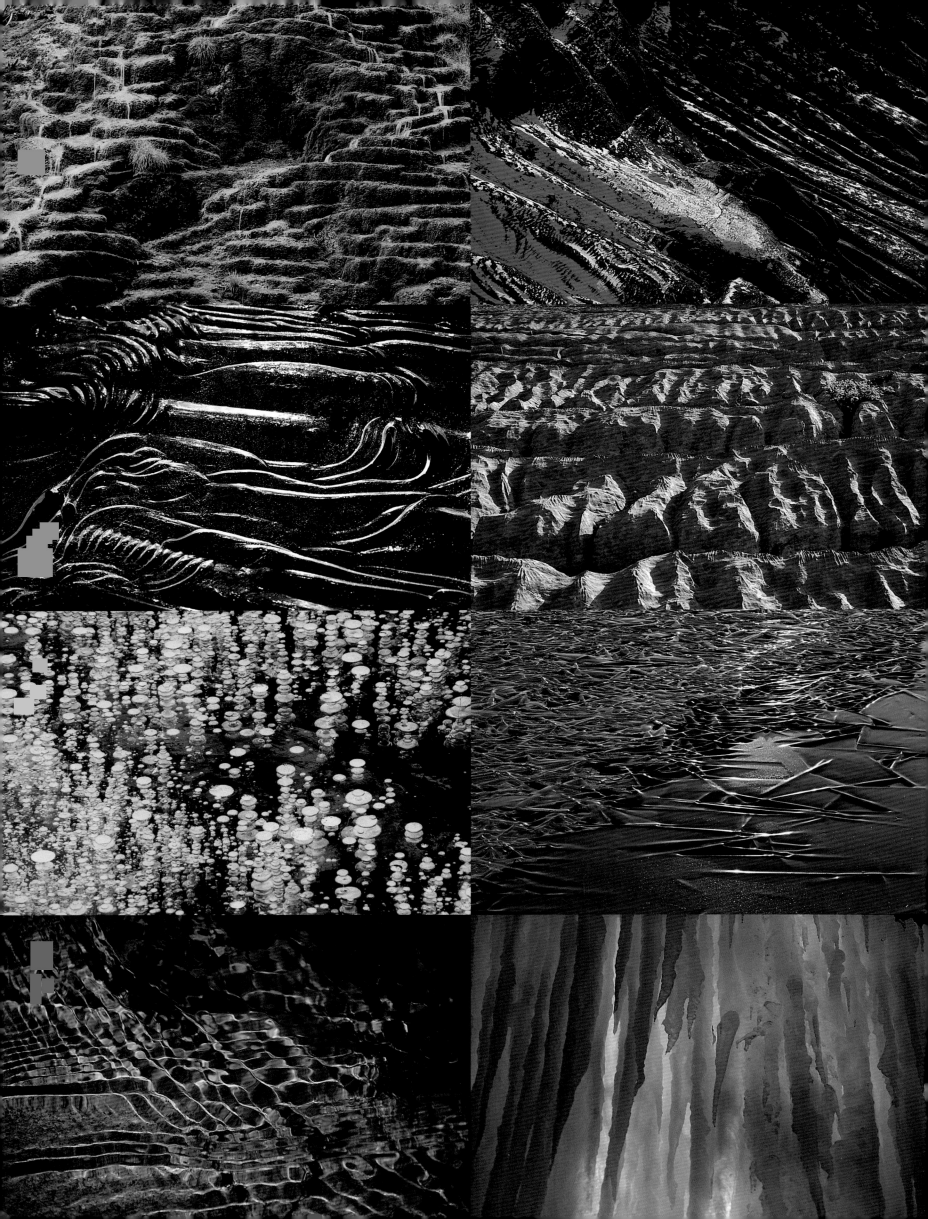

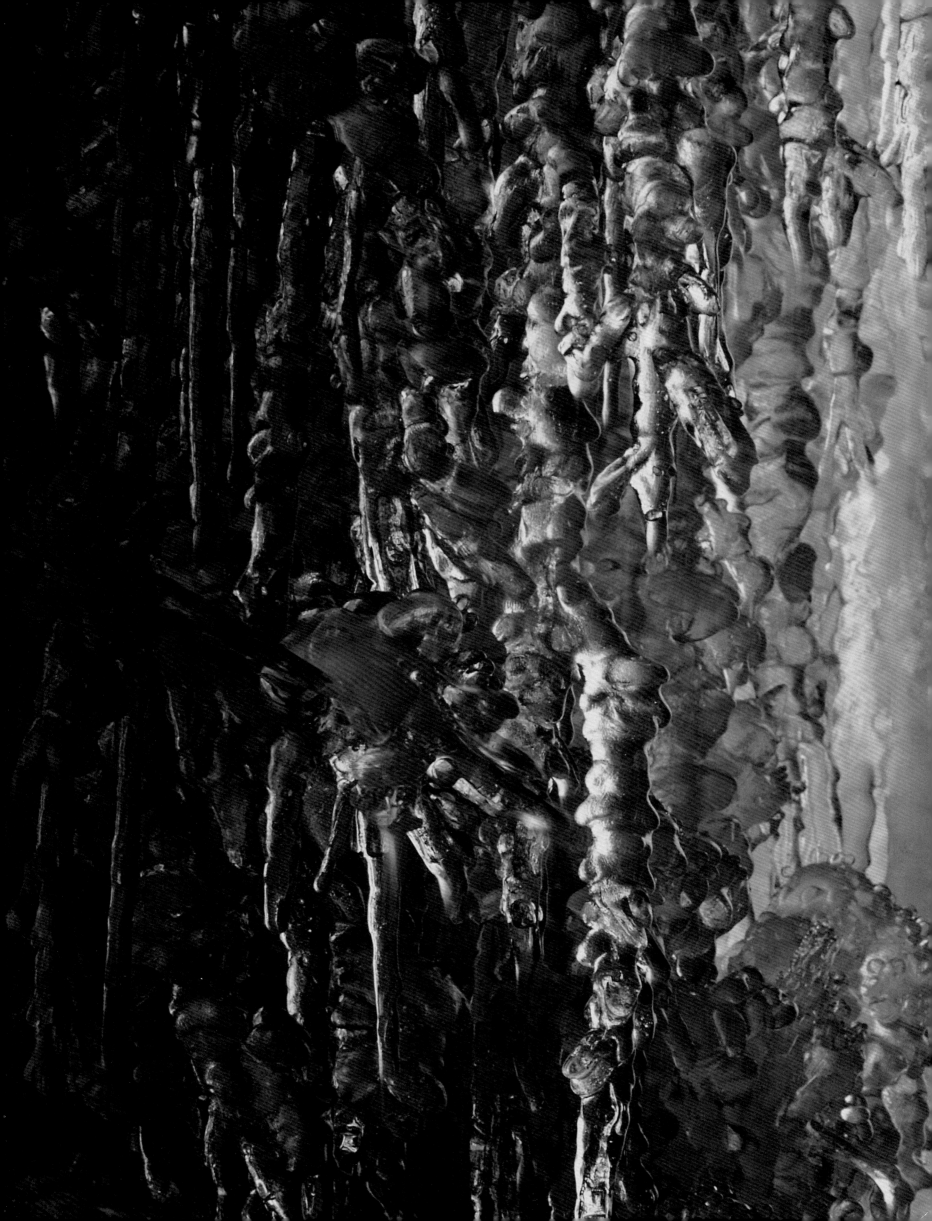

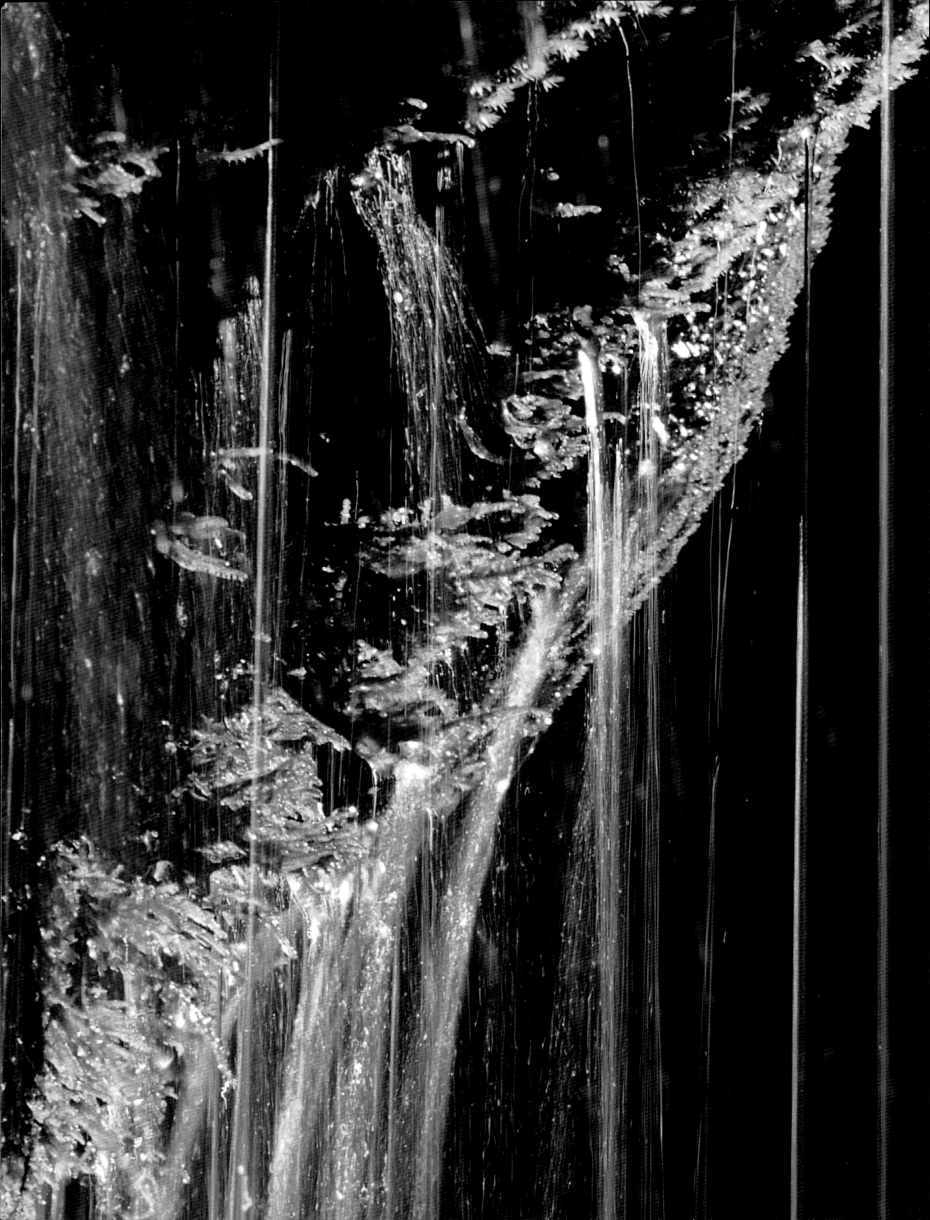

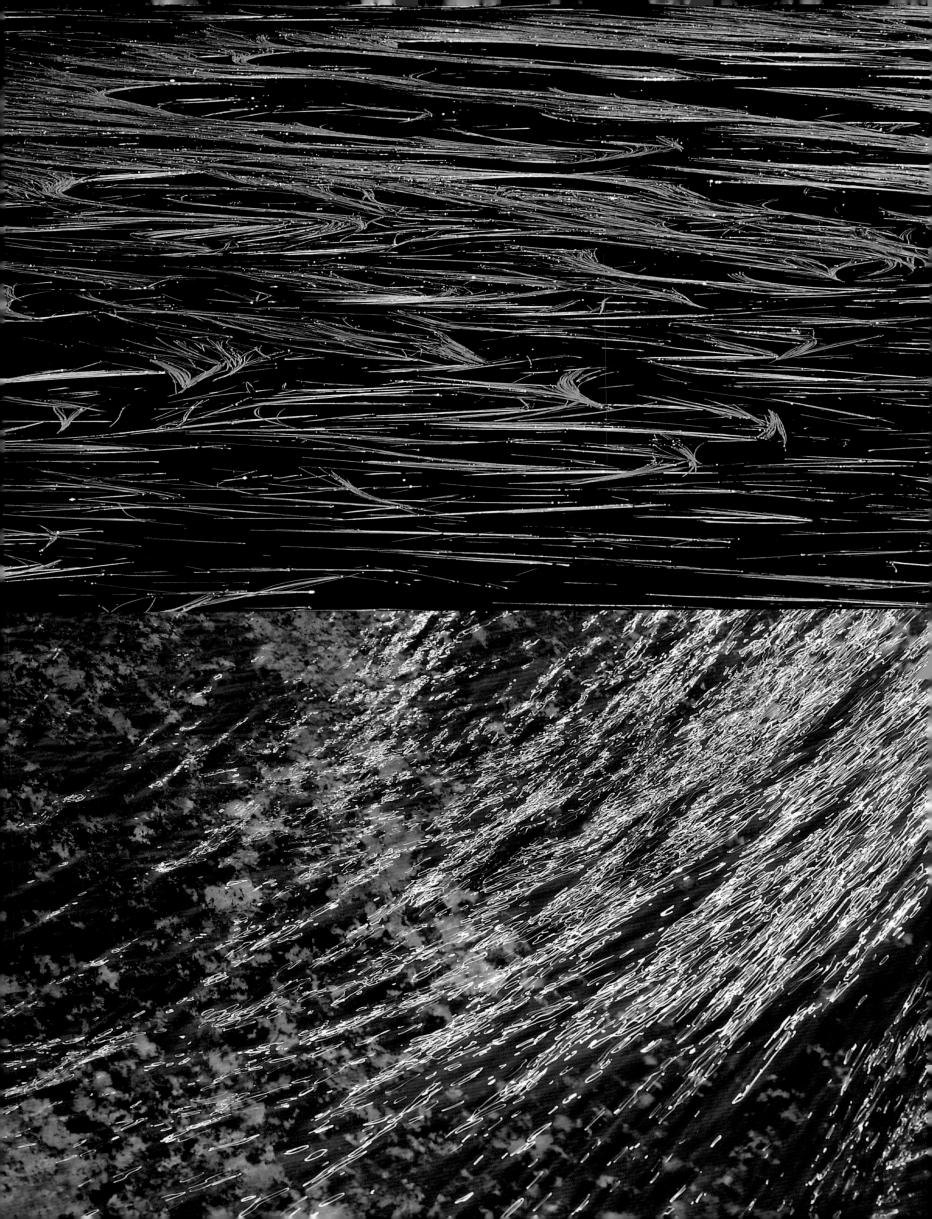

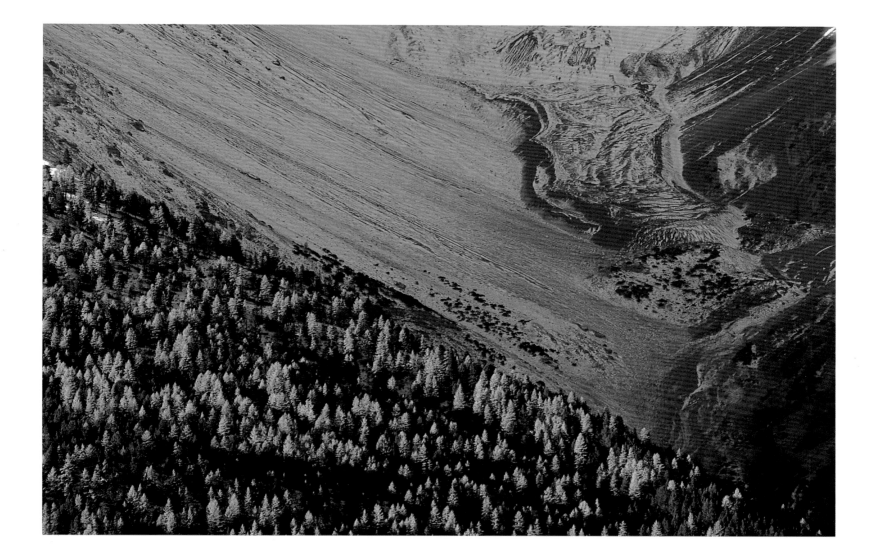

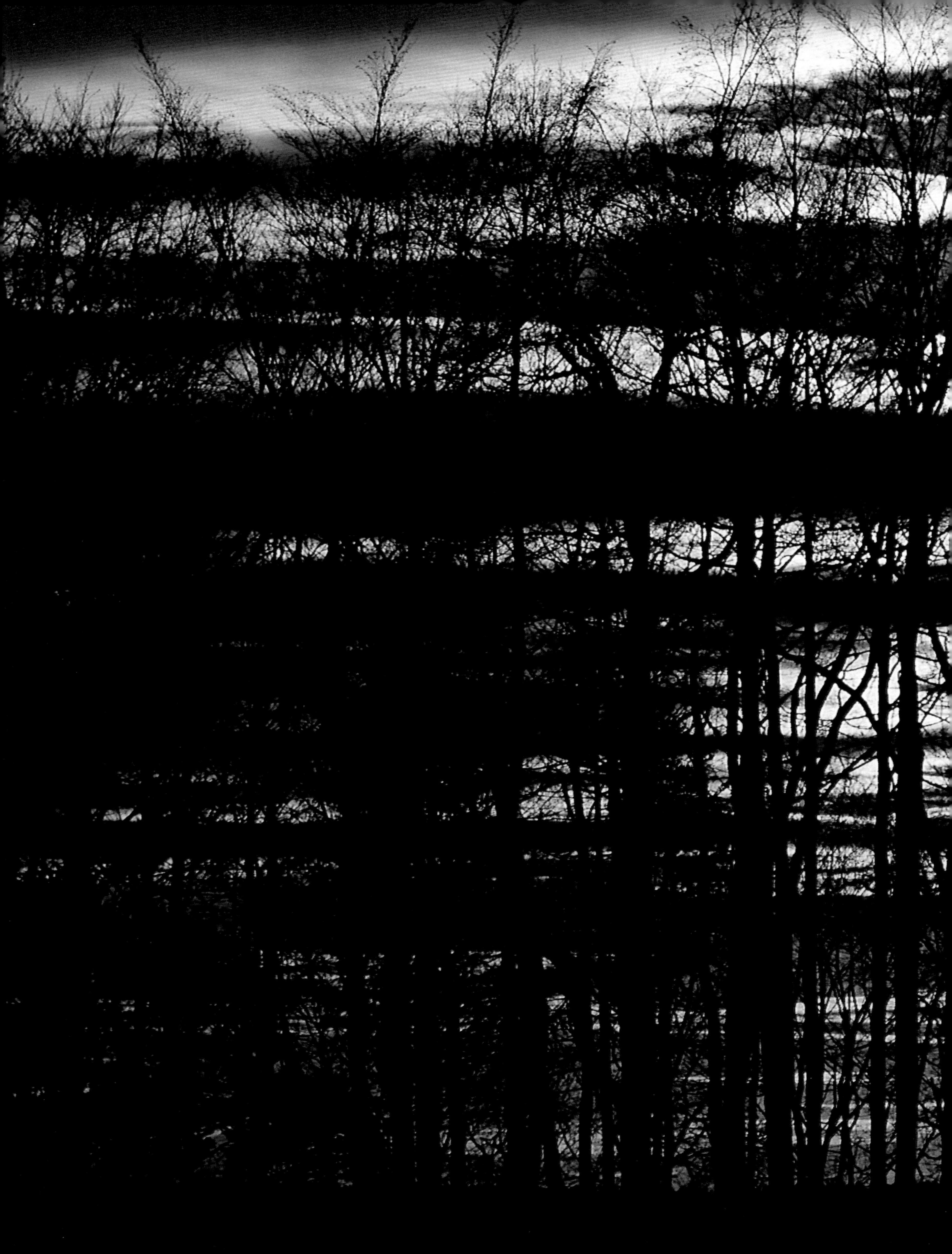

List of Illustrations

141

Val Müschauns, Grisons
Alp la Schera, national park, Grisons

Maloja, Grisons

The Stein glacier, Berne
The Rhône glacier, Valais
The Damma Massif, Berne/Valais/Uri
Granite in the Verzasca river
(near Lavartezzo), Ticino

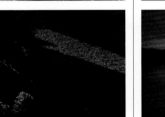

The Rhine gorge, Grisons

Moss-covered calcium precipitate deposits
Frozen mountain stream
Air pockets in the frozen surface of a lake
The flow pattern of a mountain stream
Mountain slope
Karst landscape, Glattalp, Schwyz
Ice on the lake shore
Frozen waterfall
Frozen waterfall

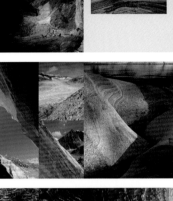

Derborence, Valais

Gental, Berne
Igls Dschimels, Bündner Alps, Grisons

Lake Lucerne with Pilatus, Lucerne/
Schwyz/Uri

Les Diablerets/Derborence, Valais

Le Soliat, Neuchâtel
Bödmerenwald, Schwyz

The Gauli glacier, Berne
Fählensee, Appenzell-Innerrhoden

Greina, Grisons
The Gauli glacier, Berne

Ice formations in the high Alps
Urbachtal, Berne

Greina, Grisons
The Morteratsch glacier, Grisons

Göscheneralp, Uri
Source of the Orbe river, Vaud

Schatzalp, Grisons
The Trümmelbach gorge, Berne

The Stein glacier, Berne
Tierberg, Berne
Albula Pass, Grisons
Brienzer Rothorn, Berne

Tössberg, Zurich
Thunersee with the Niesen, Berne
The Jungfrau Massif, Berne
Zugersee, Zug

Silberen, Schwyz
Fuorcla, Val Sassa, Grisons

Albula Pass, Grisons

145

Griessee/the Griess glacier, Valais

Alpe di Motterascio, Ticino
Bernina Pass, Grisons

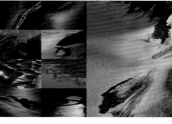

The Rhône glacier, Valais

The Stein glacier, Berne
Grimselsee, Berne

The Matterhorn, Valais
Grimselsee, Berne

Seealp, Appenzell-Innerrhoden
Rock sculptures, Viamala, Grisons
Glacial river sediment
A snowy landscape
Waterfall in the sunlight
At the foot of the mountain
Glacial deposits
Brienzersee, Berne
The Gorner glacier, Valais

Teufelskirche (Devil's Church),
Winterthur/Zurich
Forest on the Hörnli, Zurich

Reeds
Greina, Grisons
Layer of ice with air pockets
Frost flowers

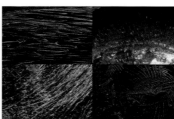

The Matterhorn, Valais
The Morteratsch glacier, Grisons

The Aletsch glacier near to the
Märjelensee, Valais

Bachalpsee and the Bernese Alps, Berne

Calcified moss
A forest in the foothills of the Alps
Calcium and algae
Lichens
Alpine succulents
Lichens
Glacial whirlpool
Lichens
An autumn leaf

The Aletsch glacier, Valais

Aelplisee (near Arosa), Grisons

Creux du Van, Neuchâtel

The Bernina Massif, Grisons

Silsersee, Grisons

Göscheneralp, Uri

The Neuchâtel Jura range, Neuchâtel

Crevices in the rock
Fählensee, Appenzell-Innerrhoden
Swathes of mist (near Arosa), Grisons
The Staubbach falls, Berne

Maggia river (near Ponte Brolla), Ticino

Hörnli with the Glarus Alps, Zurich

The Gauli falls, Berne

Primeval forest, national park, Grisons

The Gauli falls, Berne

The Fiescher glacier, Valais
Blockstrom (Permafrost), national park,
Grisons

The Rhine falls, Zurich/Schaffhausen

Alp la Schera, national park, Grisons
Furka, Uri

Rock in the Verzasca river, Ticino
Glacial sediments
Smoothed rock
Rock in the Verzasca river, Ticino

Glacier crevasse
The Jungfraujoch, Berne/Valais

The Gauli glacier, Berne
At the Seealpsee, Appenzell-Innerrhoden

Chalk terraces, Teufelskirche
(Devil's Church), Winterthur/Zurich

Karst landscape, Silberen, Schwyz
Les Diablerets, Valais

Uri Alps, Uri

Göscheneralp, Uri
Carpet la Greina, Graubünden

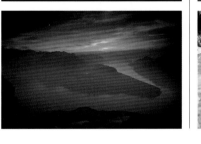

Areuse, Neuchâtel

Gyrenbad, Zurich

Frozen leaf with lichens

Lake Lucerne, Lucerne/Schwyz/Uri

Fählensee, Appenzell-Innerrhoden

Primary rocks in the Verzasca valley, Ticino

Alp la Schera, national park, Grisons

Rigi, Schwyz/Lucerne

The Matterhorn, Valais

Max Schmid

I was born on February 24th 1945 in Winterthur (Zurich). My first ten years were marked by illness and the restrictions imposed by that. Indeed, life initially showed itself to be a not entirely pleasant affair. But this was perhaps a better basis from which to nurture certain personal inclinations than might otherwise have been the case under so-called "normal" conditions.

Thanks to good nursing, I was soon restored to full health. Thereafter, a conscious perception of my physical surroundings began to develop. Very early on, geography became one of my main interests. At just ten years of age, I already owned a globe and a few maps. However, in keeping with the euphoria of that time for all that progress stood for, the atlases were limited to representations of the industrialized world that was already widely known. This was completely inadequate to satisfy my own curiosities and interests! There were too many white blank areas—vast spaces whose edges were only vaguely sketched. It was precisely these obscurely indicated land masses that awoke in me an unbridled urge to discover.

During my childhood, however, my first excursions took me only as far as my immediate surroundings—sometimes accompanied and sometimes alone. Albeit timidly, I was slowly able to translate my predilections into action within this narrow geographical framework. One blurred memory in particular comes back to me. I once embarked on a small ramble in the hilly environs of Winterthur. In the eyes of a child, though, the distance was considerable—a thoroughly courageous undertaking indeed. I was already familiar with those ponds, those willow-lined running brooks, those charming meadows on the edge of the woods. That little valley was something akin to the gateway to nature's many secrets. Up on top of the hills stood old gnarled trees in full bloom. On the distant horizon, I saw the jagged silhouette of the Alps. A high veil of cloud moving in from the west passed the zenith and lost itself over the eastern horizon in the sheer endlessness of the Eurasian continent, whose extent was, at that time, understandably not yet clear to me, it being as little known as the narrow borders of my own homeland. The sunlight filtering through the clouds bathed the world, especially this scene up on the hill, in a fairy-tale atmosphere. The sun, that moving, light-giving star, was in itself already something mysterious. But what lay hidden behind the series of horizons losing themselves in the distance? Where did these clouds come from, why were there mountains, for what reason did the sun perpetually rise and set? Question after question—which prompted my view to wander ever further over the horizon. This outing proved to be a kind of turning point for me—an experience (along with others) that set something inside me in motion. I faintly remember, though, that my coming home late didn't exactly earn me any praise ...

Another bout of illness made me want to learn more about the lands of the far North. I asked my mother to look for a book for me about the volcanic islands in the North Atlantic. I didn't want anything about Switzerland. I wanted to know all about the lands that lay beyond the earth's curvature, I wanted knowledge about where those beautifully formed, filigreed cloud formations came from. The Alps—those abrupt peaks on the far horizon—did excite my fantasy, yet even that gleaming sugared ring of mountains seemed too far out of reach. So I focused on the mountains beyond my horizon, on peaks which spewed fire, on peaks which were not easily accessible.

I did in fact receive as a present a small book about the islands on the edge of the Arctic Circle. I read about deep green oases in the midst of volcanoes and eternal ice. Finally, I knew more about them and became all the more curious to see this land with my own eyes one day. I was fascinated, and still am today, having spent years in Iceland in the meantime.

My life took the usual course with school, sports and play. Apart from geography, drawing and painting were important occupations in which I could give free expression to my love of nature in its many facets. It was only with the beginning of my professional life that these urges sank into a long slumber. Nevertheless, my professional occupation as a tiller, so alien to my impulses, proved to be a springboard back into visual art.

Like any other child of the sixties, I shared a love of music, so important to me, and that pulsating feeling of wanderlust. Because of my continuing urge to discover, however, I did not choose stereotypical travel destinations like India. What I wanted to discover had long been explored by others, but not with *my* eyes. So I set out for a land that also begins with the letter "I," a place where Northern Europeans had already settled way back in the first century. For me, this was a voyage of discovery which instilled in me the desire to travel still further.

With my first camera, I simply wanted to record what I experienced and saw. But it soon became clear to me that a camera, in the right hands, is capable of much more. Light effects and land formations, structures and situations produce miniature paintings in the viewfinder and on film. These images evolve differently than they do with a pencil or a brush. Working with the camera is, on the one hand, easier because the visual framework is defined. But on the other hand, it's much more difficult because the chosen motif is often difficult to reach and sometimes holds considerable obstacles. Together with that comes the difficult art of framing the object properly. This requires considerable energy, and external circumstances may render it complicated and occasionally turn it into a real adventure, but in the end it proves to be all the more satisfying. And this is also true, even when the photographic results don't measure up to expectations.

I was all through with being settled. Innumerable journeys to sufficiently well-known areas followed, as well as expeditions to the earth's most remote corners. At the same time, I concerned myself intensively with photography. A series of book projects took shape, dealing with different geographical locations. These included the Kerguelen, an exotic, isolated group of islands with landscapes that have been glimpsed by only a few human eyes.

The arrival of children in my life and, at the same time, an offer from a Swiss magazine, caused a long-submerged fascination to stir. Going out into the proverbial wide world in search of the unusual had made me forget the photographic potential hidden in my own backyard. While the landscapes of untouched Nature have become rare in Switzerland, they do nevertheless offer a surprising variety of motifs. To reach them often takes hard legwork. It obviously took those wide detours to the far reaches of the world, and the visual impressions gathered there, to discover or rediscover the fascinating Alpine scenery of Switzerland.

Biography

Max Schmid was born in Winterthur/Zurich on 14.2.1945. In addition to leading various photographic expeditions and travelling to the most remote areas of the world as a landscape photographer and nature-lover, he has also worked among the familiar landscapes of his homeland. His highly expressive photography has made him one of the most celebrated natural history and landscape photographers of the day. His pictures have appeared throughout the world in more than twenty lavishly illustrated books and also on various calendars.

Bibliography

1998

Kerguelen, Birkenhalde Verlag, Winterthur/Zurich, Switzerland.
Norwest USA. Nordkalifornien, Oregon, Washington, Idaho, Reich-Verlag/terra magica, Lucerne, Switzerland.

1997

USA, Reich-Verlag/terra magica, Lucerne, Switzerland.
Amerikas Naturparadiese. Die Nationalparks der USA, Reich-Verlag/terra magica, Lucerne, Switzerland.

1996

USA: Neuengland. Massachusetts, Rhode Island, Connecticut, Vermont, New Hampshire, Maine, Reich-Verlag/terra magica, Lucerne, Switzerland.
Rocky Mountains (USA). Amerikas Zauberberge, Reich-Verlag/terra magica, Lucerne, Switzerland.

1995

England, Wales, Reich-Verlag/terra magica, Lucerne, Switzerland.
Kanada, Reich-Verlag/terra magica, Lucerne, Switzerland.
Norwegen, Ellert und Richter, Hamburg, Germany.
Island, Ellert und Richter, Hamburg, Germany.

1994

London, Reich-Verlag/terra magica, Lucerne, Switzerland.
Schottland, Reich-Verlag/terra magica, Lucerne, Switzerland.
Kalifornien, Reich-Verlag/terra magica, Lucerne, Switzerland.

1993

Norwegen, Reich-Verlag/terra magica, Lucerne, Switzerland.
Finnland. Land der langen Nächte, Reich-Verlag/terra magica, Lucerne, Switzerland.
USA–Der Südwesten, Ellert und Richter, Hamburg, Germany.
Irland, Ellert und Richter, Hamburg, Germany.

1992

Dänemark, Reich-Verlag/terra magica, Lucerne, Switzerland.

1991

Island, Ellert und Richter, Hamburg, Germany.
Die Anden, Reich-Verlag/terra magica, Lucerne, Switzerland.

1990

Grönland. Naturparadies im Norden, Reich-Verlag/terra magica, Lucerne, Switzerland.

1989

Neuseeland. Land der langen weißen Wolke, Reich-Verlag/terra magica, Lucerne, Switzerland.
Irland, Reich-Verlag/terra magica, Lucerne, Switzerland.

1985

Island–Exotik des Nordens, Iceland Review, Reykjavik, Iceland.

1981

Faszination Landschaft, Verlag Photographie, Schaffhausen, Switzerland.

159

Translation from the German by Havard Davies, Ann-Marie Michel
Editorial direction by Sara Schindler
Layout and Typography by Guido Widmer, Zurich, Switzerland
Printed by Kündig Druck AG, Baar/Zug, Switzerland
Bound by Buchbinderei Burkhardt AG, Mönchaltorf/Zurich, Switzerland

SPONSOR
This book has been sponsored by **Siemens Building Technologies AG,**
Zurich, Switzerland, "a Siemens Group company."

ISBN 3-908161-36-3